Frank James Jr.

The Gifted Leader

The Gifted Leader

ISBN: 978-1-7368307-0-3 1st Ed.

TJF Productions

Lansing, MI. 48911

For Permissions, contact:

thegiftedleaderfj@gmail.com

𝒯able of 𝒞ontents

Dedication

This book is dedicated to my heart and soul, my family! Jenifer, Izayah and Zy'Aire. I love you all with every fiber of my being and my only hope is that I made you all proud with the work that I have done in leadership both in this book and in real life!

Sincerely,

Your Gifted Leader!

Hubby and Daddy.

Leaders, the energy you give off is powerful! People can feel when they are being tolerated instead of celebrated. Find the good in your team, or they will find the smallest flaw in you and make it big.

NOW GO AND BE GIFTED!

-Frank James Jr.

Forward

The role of a leader can often be misconstrued as simply a title one holds within a company or a household. Although this idea holds some truth, holding the title merely speaks to a position and not the posture of true leadership. A position is a declaration of placement, while posture depicts the behavior and attitude of those that uphold the role. Many of us have accepted the position as a leader but have struggled to grasp the totality of what true leadership encompasses. We have been living in this false narrative of what and who a leader is for far too long, but that ends today! Today you will embark on a new journey of becoming, The Gifted Leader. The word journey is utilized intentionally to emphasize that being, The Gifted Leader, requires a life-long commitment to both absorption and reproduction.

The Gifted Leader

The Gifted Leader is a power packed resource manual for individuals who believe they have the gift to lead. The dynamic author, Frank James Jr, utilizes his personal experiences to enhance one's knowledge of the multifaceted realm of leadership and provides you the necessary tools to harness and utilize your gift to its fullest capacity. Frank strategically intertwines complexity and simplicity in his depiction of leadership tools within this manual. The complexity will challenge your psyche, while the simplicity will allow for complete absorption of this profound perspective of leadership. This perspective was birthed through triumphs and failures that have afforded Frank the opportunity to not only enhance his gift but to recognize and cultivate the gift in others. In this book, you will learn the importance of vulnerability, how to address crises in the chaos, and the most powerful tool you possess, reproduction.

The Gifted Leader and The Gifted Leader Workbook provide you with the necessary leadership tools to not only enhance your leadership style but to cultivate the leader in others. This book is for both the expert and the novice. If you desire to catapult your leadership style and take on the commission to cultivate the leadership in others, I challenge you to embrace the tools, even when it seems like a personal dagger. I believe the book was written with the intention to trim off the unnecessary, so the muscles of leadership can break forth. Thank you, Frank, for this has truly sparked my inner leader.

Jenifer N James, LPC, CCTP, CAADC

President,

The Storehouse

Intro

Webster defines leading as "The innate ability to make an informed logical decision". (Merriam-Webster & Inc., 2019) There are so many things that come to mind when you think about a topic as broad as leadership. I find more often than not that leadership can be looked at in several different ways. It is not by mistake that when we think of a job, we are very quick to make a judgment on whether the boss or manager is good. This is usually done before even seeing their leadership in action. It's usually emotionally charged (both good and bad) and oftentimes inaccurate. I would like to submit this new idea to you; Leadership is a lifestyle and ultimately a gift!

Frank James Jr.

When I enter a room, I am not on a quest or mission to get people to merely just agree with me, I want to shift their perspectives. Some people view that as cocky or arrogant and others view it as "Frank is always trying to be the leader of something". While that is what people say outwardly, I believe what they are actually experiencing is my gift operating in their presence. When you are gifted to lead, it is incredibly important for you to understand how you show up and how you are received. I am always sensitive to the notion that when I show up, there are usually three different things that can happen in the room. First, there are a group of leaders who get inspired. Secondly, there are a group of leaders that may feel slightly intimidated and finally, there are a group of leaders who are uninterested in being present. Your sensitivity to surveying the room accurately is key to navigating your connection and flow within the room.

Leaders have to be able to juggle a myriad of things and still operate with the intent to shift perspectives. I use the word gift and I am sure that probably has you thinking it was a misuse of that word. However, I am going to submit to you several different principles that I hope will show you how leadership is a gift to both the giver and receiver. A person with the gift of leadership exudes an energy that can be experienced in many different ways. When most people think about leadership, it is usually in the realm of leadership as an occupation, not a gift. Through this book, I am going to dissect a few characteristics and perspectives on how to exercise your gift of leadership. Together, we will explore the idea of leadership being a gift by focusing on the seven principles of gifted leadership:

1) Attitude of Leadership

2) Burdens of Perfection

3) Vulnerability/Transparency/Intentionality

4) Tough Choices and Hard Conversations

5) The Follow up

6) Influence

7) Cultivating Gifts

If you will allow me the opportunity to share both real life experiences and direct information from the spirit, I can promise you it will help you make the necessary adjustments to your leadership style and ultimately become a gifted leader. Please hear me when I say, I am only an expert in the many experiences that I will share with you. However, if the gift is in you this is my attempt to draw it out of you. There may be some things that sound familiar to you. I encourage you to take all that you need from every principle and use it to catapult you into the greatest leader that you have been gifted to be.

Your level of skill does not depict your level of leadership. If you are incredibly knowledgeable but lack empathy, you in fact are not a leader at all. You are merely just a person in charge.

NOW GO AND BE GIFTED!

-Frank James Jr.

Chapter 1

Attitude of Leadership

Have you ever heard the saying "your attitude will determine your aptitude"? I know I have heard that many times and I always wondered exactly what people were trying to express. I came up with many definitions of what I thought this meant and I was able to land at one which I will share but let me tell you a story first. Early on my Leadership Attitude was activated. Growing up in the inner city of Detroit, I was fortunate enough to be surrounded by a large portion of my very closely knit family. One of the fondest memories I have as a child was the annual family trip we would take to Cedar Point Amusement Park in Sandusky Ohio. I can't recall a year where we did not take this family trip. This yearly trip was so profound for me in more ways than I knew then. I learned that I have an ultimate love for this industry and that resulted in my working in it for many years. What I remember about those trips was the projected arrival time and departure time. It was conveyed to us many times leading up to the date of the trip that if you were not on time you would be left. Subsequently if you were not on the bus to head home you would then be left at the park. Now with this being family, I couldn't imagine that anyone would have ever been left, but because of the posture of my aunt, who organized the trip, I was not willing to test the theory.

I usually took the leadership role with my group of cousins and planned out the entire day at the park. I will admit that most of the time, lunch or stopping to eat were never part of the plans. I had one thing on my mind; we have to be RIDE WARRIORS, riding everything before the park closes. In the early years, I would get into arguments with my cousins because they felt like my plan was unrealistic and ultimately something that they didn't want to do. It came to a point that we eventually separated, and I enjoyed the park on my own. When we returned to the bus, I remember vividly that everybody was filled with excitement and discussed what their experience was at the park that day. One year, I was fortunate enough to ride every thrill attraction in the park and in some cases, rode a few of them twice. I even had the photos to prove it. So as everyone was sharing their stories, I stayed quiet and listened to them speak. The cousins that I used to ride with had unfortunately ridden 6 of the 17 large roller coasters. When it became my turn to speak, I shared that I had ridden every ride in the park. Of course, in true family fashion, this was met with opposition and accusations of untruth. Once I showed the photos, the conversation changed a bit. "Well how did you ride everything and why didn't you go with us?" they asked.

At that moment one thing became very clear to me. This was a direct and real-life example of your attitude determining your aptitude. I begged them to allow me to show them how we should tackle the park in a methodical way, in order to get the optimum results. They refused, rejected and even came up with a plan to, "lose me and be on their own", so that I wouldn't control their fun. What they did not know was that I studied the park and because I met no strangers, I talked to many employees that worked there. I had the plans down to a science. Start at the back, skip the middle and go to the front for lunch. Then do the middle last because people will be waiting in lines for the big rides that you had already ridden. Like magic, that worked! Before I could describe my plans to them, it started a fight and an argument, so I made the decision to go at it alone. The results paid off and to this day, they are still perplexed on how I was able to make that happen. Their direct attitude and disposition regarding the trip cost them an experience that they regret. This happens very often in leadership.

When you are gifted to lead, it is important that you understand and study situations. One of the factors that separate good leaders from gifted leaders is the ability to see the larger picture as well as the small details. It is not by accident that people who are gifted to lead are usually critical thinkers. It is the nature of our mindset to find the problem, dissect the problem and then fix it. One of the challenges I was faced with on the bus was, the inability to share both my thoughts and insights as to why I did what I did. Explaining the why behind situations can go a long way. In leadership, there will be moments that you don't have time to explain the why, but you must remember to circle back to ensure you are not leaving your team behind or in the dark. A gifted leader NEVER leaves their team in the dark and always brings them along the journey. This is not to say that there won't be things that the team is not privy to. However, when you need a task completed efficiently and effectively, disclosure is necessary for the ultimate end goal. Here are a few things you should ask yourself and your team when you are working towards completing a task:

1. What is the task that needs to be completed?
2. What is the deadline for completion?
3. What information is pertinent for your success?
4. How do I encourage, support and hold everyone accountable?
5. What is my team's understanding of what I am asking of them?

When you are dealing with people, asking them for understanding can sometimes be a challenge. When I give directions, I always end it with "what is it that I am asking of you?" Oftentimes individuals become offended when asked that question because they view it as condescending. While it can truly be a condescending question, you must be able to understand your audience and communicate in a way that is clear. It's so important for your team to understand both your direction and your intent. This is built through trust and vulnerability by both the leader and the team. Many people use the notion that they don't want a boss, they want a leader. What they are essentially saying is, they do not want to be controlled. One thing to keep in mind is the understanding of what controlling is. Control is simply leadership without communication. Respectfully, the leader is "in control" but your ability to communicate in such a way that is clear, understood, and dynamic, is truly a characteristic that a gifted leader must possess. A gifted leader must be a leader in both word and action. Understand that you are not attached to a company or a position; you are attached to your gift; which is designed to make room for you wherever you go.

Leaders make mistakes — OWN THEM! Excellence takes a level of failure. Be vulnerable enough as a leader to fail and brave enough to create an environment that is safe enough for others to fail. It is from this place, where gifted leaders emerge.

NOW GO AND BE GIFTED!

-Frank James Jr.

Chapter 2

The Burdens of Perfection

As a leader, you are often met with the anxiety of meeting deadlines, making tough decisions, having hard conversations and accepting accountability. With these things alone, it can cause one to go into a state of self-perfection. When you are gifted to lead, one of the many standouts that always reside in you is the ability to do a great job and perform well. I can't think of any leader that doesn't want to do a great job and be impactful. While as a leader you are committed to excellence, there are some burdens that come along with being perfect. It reminds me of a story of one of my past career changes.

As I shared earlier, Amusement Parks was my career of choice and passion for the vast majority of my life. Once I graduated from college, I made a career change into the food service industry. I began working at a fast-food establishment, where I aggressively climbed the ladder. I remember being told during the interview for the position, "we have this audit that we get 3 times a year and all you need to know is that failing it is not an option." That was not only the brunt of the conversation, it was the entire conversation. Naturally, I prioritized this aspect within my training to ensure I met the sentiments my manager discussed and ensure a passing score. I will never forget my second day on the job. Here I am only four hours into my shift and the auditor walks in. Yes, this was the audit that my boss warned me about. I greeted her at the front counter, invited her back and then communicated to the proper channels that she had arrived.

Frank James Jr.

As she entered the back of the house, I asked if I could walk with her so that I could learn the process and she obliged. She began by taking food temperatures and the second temperature she took was non-compliant resulting in an immediate assessment failure. We were not even 5 minutes into the assessment and we had already failed. I started to internalize this and made it my fault. I remember saying to myself, "Frank why didn't you check those and have someone else check them? Why didn't you create a checklist to ensure things were double checked? Why would you fail this audit on your second day, you very well may be fired today"? Now let's pause here for a second before we continue on with the story. There are a few things to consider here when it comes to leadership. That line of questioning that I had within myself is something that I believe most leader's experience. Usually, it does not stop there. You continue to go on, asking even more questions but nothing satisfies your feeling of failure. This outcome was one that you had not anticipated or prepared for. I call that the perfection complex.

You must know that at any given time, things can go wrong or unplanned and you must remain focused, present and have the ability to regroup.

Once she told me that the temperature was non-compliant and I had that internal moment of huge conflict, my boss walked in. Great timing, right? Yes! God truly does have a great sense of humor. She looked at my face and asked what happened. I began to explain to her that we had already failed and how sorry I was for not completing my one job, which was passing this audit. Before I get to her response, I think it's important to note what my tasks were for that day. As a new employee, the first two weeks is spent training on the computer learning the business. You do not touch the floor at all until you learn "the basics". I had been in an office on a computer watching videos for the past two days and had zero control over what was happening within the restaurant. I did not even consider that my responsibilities for the day were only to learn. Internally, I beat myself up badly and then I had to figure out how best to explain what happened to my boss.

While in the midst of explaining, she said "Frank, stop it. What are you talking about? You have not even been here two days and you think this is your fault? No, that's what the other managers should have been doing while you were learning." I said OK and I continued walking with the auditor and learning the process. It was such a great experience that I later began working for the company, but I will discuss this later. First, let's dissect the "perfection complex" and how it relates to the burdens of perfection.

Most people when completing something that will be on display, really desire to do a good job. Typically, people don't wake up asking "just how mediocre or subpar can I be today?" On the contrary, they either wake up already motivated or get into their motivation routine and set off on a journey to do something spectacular. While everything that you attach your name to should be done in excellence, you must always allow yourself room for failure and regrouping. Not allowing yourself to have a down moment, creates an environment that is not only stressful, but it is unworkable and causes great internal and external conflict. As a leader, it is pertinent that while you want your team to succeed, you should always acknowledge the possibility of failure. That may sound weird, but without failure you are truly not growing. When delegating tasks and the subsequent follow up, your response is critical to understand when something or someone comes up short. There are three quick actions that a gifted leader can take without falling prey to the burdens of perfections. I call this the AR^2 method; Analyze, Resolve, Reset! Let's talk about the first component of the AR^2 method, Analyze.

When a task has fallen short, the first thing you need to do is analyze the problem. Analyzing the problem begins with the instructions given. You will find that in many situations, the end result is usually problematic because of the individual's misinterpretation of instructions. It is imperative that instructions are clear and concise. A gifted leader understands that it is unfair to hold someone accountable for a lack of understanding with unclear instructions. This plays a key role in ensuring that communication with the leader is fluid. When writing instructions, it is very important that you gather feedback on how the instructions are both written and interpreted. One thing that I have learned in leadership is the importance of soliciting feedback based on instructional understanding. When feedback is presented as a part of your regular conversation, it is usually received both well and effective. As I mentioned, I always give the instruction first and then ask, "can you explain to me what it is that I am asking of you?" Now I will say, doing this as a result of an issue can create a bit of hostility which is why I always do it in the planning phase.

Once you have gauged that they understand what the task is, you are clear to let them spread their wings and fly. When analyzing what went wrong, it is good to state "When we started you were able to tell me exactly what the task was, where did we go wrong?" Emphases on the use of the word we. While it may have been the misfortune of one person's task in part or in whole, leaders are responsible for everything that takes place. This is why it's important to lean on your toolbox of gifts, in order to protect the safe space that you have created for yourself and your team. The components of this conversation provide the foundation for the building block of Resolve.

The difference between a leader and one who is gifted to lead is the innate ability to respond in a way that not only gets results but facilitates complete understanding. Getting results without resolve is a recipe for meeting an exact issue for a second time. It can be incredibly frustrating to both the team and the leader when there is a situation that is constantly being repeated. Resolve can be defined as the solution to an existing problem. Sometimes this resolution requires multiple attempts at both analyzing the problem and the resolution step. In leadership, the process that it takes for one to discover a solution can be described as insight. A person who is gifted to lead has both insight and foresight. Insight is the keen ability to accurately understand the premise of a person or situation. As defined by Webster, foresight is the ability to predict what will be needed in the future and be able to create the means for resolution even before the problem arises. (Merriam-Webster & Inc., 2019) When a leader is met with an issue in need of a resolution, insight is usually the go to tool used to ascertain and correct the issue. What I tend to find in many instances are that some leaders only act on insight while foresight serves as an afterthought. Using these two together can be dynamic when interacting with a team or yourself in many ways.

When I was hired as the General Manager of an Indoor Amusement Park, I was told that the team was long tenured and desired to do well. Ultimately, they just were not doing enough for the owners to feel comfortable with "letting them do it all". After posing many questions to the owners, it became very clear to me that the team needed to be completely revamped.   There was an evident lack of leadership presence and unfortunately when there is no true leadership, major resistance to change is common. I spent the better part of my first two months terminating and hiring.

What a ride that was! When I finally had the opportunity to begin to dive into some of the shortcomings, what I found was the manager running the park lacked foresight and had very limited insight. Her insight was so limited that it resulted in not knowing the right questions to ask in order to gain a better understanding of the needs and wants of the owners. In my opinion, it was the true definition of, "I am just here to pick up my paycheck". So, after spending some time with her and imparting some things to help both her insight and foresight we became an unstoppable team. Together, we had to resolve many inconsistencies within the facility in order to get on the better side of things. Resolution is something that is often seen as the final step in mastering an issue, when in reality it is not. Reset is the final step.

When I hear the word reset, there are a few things that come to mind. The first is the thought of another chance to knock the results out of the ballpark. Next, is the frustration of having to start over and not getting it corrected the first time? Finally, I think about the myriad of ways I can make it bigger and better with the foresight that I gained going through the process. There are things that gifted leaders truly enjoy about going through a process more than one time. For example, I work in a third-party health and brand standard organization, where we do assessments for many different companies. Yes, if you are wondering, this is the same company that I spoke about earlier that completed audits. However, this time I happened to be on the giving end of the audit. In order to progress in any way in this company, there is an exam that you must pass. Going into this exam I felt both prepared and anxious. I was told that as soon as I had passed the exam, that the sky was the limit for me in selecting an advancement opportunity. I took the exam and failed it by two points. I was livid! I couldn't believe that all the time I spent studying meant nothing and I failed so miserably. I wanted to crawl away, disconnect and quit. I assumed immediately that I was going to be stuck in my current position, unable to be promoted. However, I analyzed what my shortcomings were, resolved my issue, reset my thought process and aced the exam the second time.

After having that experience, I was promoted immediately and had many co-workers ask me about the exam. I could have shared my initial thoughts about being unprepared and how awful the exam was. Being a gifted leader, I instead thought to myself, how do I use this moment to make a positive impact in the life of someone who is going to embark on this same mission? In retrospect, while this was an incredibly difficult exam, it was the way in which the questions were worded that ultimately stumped me. I used that insight to not only propel myself to success, but I began to share this insight with anyone who would listen. In this instance, I had to really tap into my influence as a gifted leader and realize that as much as I didn't want to fail the test or take it again, I gained some really great knowledge in the process. That knowledge and insight enabled me to reset my focus and enter a second time levelheaded. When you reset, you have to forget the feeling, but remember the process. Going into a situation with the emotional attachment inhibits your ability to pull forth the knowledge and skills you need to make changes moving forward. Don't be a leader that takes a hit and then loses it. Be the leader that takes the hit and then recovers. You are gifted to bounce back.

Leaders, when you do things for credit, it skews your result. Instead, focus on engaging people's journey and enhancing their strengths. When you make personal deposits into people's lives, you won't be on a search for credit. It will come automatically in how they move afterwards.

NOW GO AND BE GIFTED!

-Frank James Jr.

Chapter 3

Vulnerability / Transparency & Intentionality

Vulnerability, Transparency and Intentionality are three of the most daring characteristics that a leader can both possess and exude. Any situation, no matter how large or small, requires the use of one or all of these characteristics at some point. It is the divine capability to effectively move within these characteristics that really help to set apart gifted leaders. Vulnerability is a conscious choice not to hide your emotions or desires from others despite the risk of physical or emotional harm or attack. (Merriam-Webster & Inc., 2019) I must be honest, when I first read that definition; I began to question whether or not I could be vulnerable with my team. Did I have the capacity to be vulnerable for the sake of effective leadership? I had an internal conflict of push back and rejection, until I was reminded of its relevance during the 2020 Global Pandemic.

As a result of this Pandemic, the Executive Leadership Team was tasked with revamping procedures in order to stabilize revenue during this difficult time. I received a phone call from one of the leaders, of whom I respect greatly, and I was once their mentee, and he said, "I need you to create a virtual process for what we do in person daily. I need the SOP written, the process tested, all pertinent parties contacted within the company and then a proof of concept on my desk within a week, can you handle that?" Of course, I said yes! I was grateful to be called upon but after I said yes, I experienced what I would describe as a reckless loss for words. I had so many questions including the most obvious one, "where do I start?" It was at that moment that I had to exercise the idea of vulnerability into my leadership style. I sat for a moment and asked myself, why did he ask me? Then I realized that sometimes people can sense who you are and call on your gift. There was nothing special or spectacular that I had done besides allow my gift to show up in any room that I entered. It is always my goal to shift the perspective of every room and sometimes that gets a little tricky to navigate.

I made it to the point of presenting the first draft to individuals within the company and it was a failure. In my opinion, it was ripped to shreds. While no one seemingly said anything negative, their feedback or coaching points were related to items that were not accessible to me. I felt judged and ultimately like I had truly failed! This was weighing on me heavily as I felt like this was my opportunity to really shine and show just how precise I could be. However, after processing the situation, I realized that I merely needed to engage my vulnerability. Anytime you put something on display for others to view and process, you must understand that judgment is an enemy to your vulnerability. This process that I was experiencing was for me to not only gain exposure in many departments, but it was also to help me understand that when leading you have to learn when to divorce the idea of receiving credit, to obtain the best outcome possible.

During this process I had to sit in numerous meetings where I had to provide and receive transparent feedback in order to produce the most dynamic material possible. Transparency: the inability to hide or conceal anything; showing oneself and your limitations. (Merriam-Webster & Inc., 2019) When I began training the teams on the new procedures, I was transparent about my knowledge limits even though I was the creator of the format. I believe my transparency and willingness to be vulnerable during the process of development, aided in the smooth transition for both myself and colleagues. Questions arose requiring me to respond with, "I didn't think about that, let me work that out with my team and circle back." It is a myth that a leader will know absolutely everything about every topic. I believe we discount the human factor of people when we judge leaders based off of them not knowing something. This is why it is so important that as a gifted leader, you are very intentional about everything that you do.

Individuals want to be engaged, respected, uplifted, and appreciated. One of the errors that we often make as leaders is incorrectly navigating the engagement process. It is incredibly important to be intentional about bringing people, "along for the ride," instead of just giving instructions and dropping them off at a bus stop with the expectation of grand results. Being vulnerable, transparent and intentional does not make you a weak leader; on the contrary it makes you a brave leader. One who is effectively focused on operating in their gift of leadership. There have been many situations where there was not a definitive path to achieve my desired goals. The truth is, there can and will be many situations whereas the leader, you must create your own path. It is in these moments, that it is imperative that you rely on your instincts and be intentional about both the choices and decisions that you make. I recall a time when I accepted a management position that placed me in charge of several team members who had also applied for the same position. I intentionally spent time with each of them and encouraged them to share their frustrations about the series of events.

At first, because I was now their direct report, you can imagine they were incredibly apprehensive about sharing how they felt about the decisions, in fear of retaliation. With this in mind, I made it a point and a purpose to have an environment that was open for them to share without the fear of retaliation. I finally got one of them to open up and I remember her asking me "What do you want man? Why do you keep asking me how I feel? Why do you care anyway, you got the job?" At that moment, I had to exhibit empathy towards her. I allowed her to freely express her true feelings in order to arrive at the place of coexistence within the company. Although I am the leader of the team, I still needed both her and her gift to show up. I believe due to my approach, something clicked for her. By truly showing an interest in how she was feeling, and not minimizing or dismissing her feelings, it truly paved the way for a great working relationship. We worked together for several years after that. I was given one of the most profound compliments I had ever received from my experience working with her. She said to me, "I see why they hired you and not me".

In that moment, my commitment to vulnerability, transparency, and intentionality as a leader was validated. Let's face it; failing is simply part of the leading process. At some point during your tenure as a leader, there will be something that goes well and then something that fails. When you fail, it is your responsibility as a leader to be intentional about being vulnerable and transparent. Usually, we try to cover up our faults and mishaps quickly. However, we learned earlier in this book that there is a methodical process (AR^2) that a leader should enact to ensure that they do not fall prey to the burdens of perfection or repeated process of failure. As we cypher through this concept of vulnerability, transparency and intentionality there will be things that will cause some internal push back. I urge you to welcome that feeling and allow it to change how you do leadership. Don't fall prey to pride or not wanting to look bad. It clouds your ability to be a gifted leader.

Leaders, hard conversations are part of the job. If you want people to receive you, put in their formula of communication. The message never changes, but the delivery should be personalized always.

NOW GO AND BE GIFTED!

-Frank James Jr.

Chapter 4

Tough Choices / Hard Conversations

It is inevitable that as a leader you will encounter tough choices and hard conversations on a regular basis. It is your innate ability to maneuver through these choices and conversations that set you apart as a gifted leader. It is often said that leaders should not make emotional decisions. It must strictly be about business. I would like to offer a counter to that thought. There is a mantra that I have adapted to my current leadership style: I am here to do two things; educate and regulate. When deciding how to best deal with an uncomfortable conversation it is extremely important that emotions from both parties are taken into consideration. The ability to include the emotional aspect of others will aid in progressing the conversation and decision forward.

One of the most challenging times in my leadership tenure occurred when I accepted the General Manager's position of an indoor Amusement Park. As a young manager, I had to demonstrate my ability to balance both business and emotion when it related to dealing with my staff, as many of them were teenagers. This alone brought its own set of unique experiences to undertake. I remember first having the interview and being asked "the salary that you are requesting is pretty high, what are you going to do to make that kind of money?" I immediately responded with "I'm a game changer!" At the time, I shared that my philosophy was to run a tight ship and make it safely to the destination. While I have not moved far from that philosophy, I had to learn to make several adjustments in the way that I moved as a leader. I had to learn to tap into my gift.

As both the General Manager and newest employee, I was tasked with the responsibility to revamp the staff in an effort to draw in both new customers as well encourage former customers to return. This task required that I make drastic leadership and managerial moves throughout the park. Initially, I viewed this task as a "quick fix" and began game planning. Very quickly, however, I learned that my seemingly quick fix would be anything but quick. To effectively revamp the park, I thought it advantageous to analyze where we were as a team and how we arrived there. The goal being to resolve and reset. In the midst of doing this, the AR^2 Leadership method was implemented. Despite successfully revamping the park, the owners ultimately decided that separation of some staff members was necessary. As the GM, the tough conversations were a part of my job.

Prior to speaking with the current manager, I was fully prepared to have the extremely tough conversion. It was my plan to inform her that she was being let go but something had shifted. As we spoke, she shared her observations of the level of engagement and influence that I had with the owners which she was unable to obtain. She explained how difficult and sometimes impossible it was to make some of the decisions that I did because it was always met with opposition. She went on to share how she was working to care for her family. She was a single mother and she depended on this job. Now, at this moment I was stuck! I felt like I was caught in the middle of a battle of will and skill. I kept telling myself, Frank, take the emotion out and be a boss. Then something changed in me. I realized that having emotion as a leader is first normal and secondly, appropriate. I utilized that emotion to help create a better leader in myself and her. It assisted me in the game planning process and ultimately catapulted her knowledge and skill level as a leader. When I think about that story in retrospect, I often find myself wondering, what if I had made the wrong decision that day? Could I have ruined someone's life due to my refusal to not factor emotions into my decisions?

Emotions are valuable. As a leader, you have to ensure that they play a role in the decision but not be the driving force behind it. One of the things that I admire about

the world renown Author and Counselor, Brene' Brown, is her work in leadership and vulnerability. One thing that she makes abundantly known is, when you are a leader you must be very clear with your words and actions. She made a statement that changed the paradigm of my leadership style forever, "Clear is kind, unclear is unkind". (Brown, 2018) When I first heard this listening to her audiobook, I thought hmm, I wonder what she is going to go into. Through my research, I found that when you are amidst a tough conversation or a hard choice, it's extremely important that you are absolutely clear about intentions, solutions and next steps. As a leader, you will have to decide on plenty of situations where the most appropriate decision is one that is not necessarily in favor of yourself or sometimes, the people you are leading. Understanding that the balls and strikes have to be called accordingly, the way in which you handle them sets you apart as a gifted leader. There are going to be things that come up, that you may have never dealt with before. It is imperative that you understand, it is your gift of leadership that is being summoned. You can do it!

Leaders, the follow up is nonnegotiable. It is the one place where you can correct and adjust.

NOW GO AND BE GIFTED!

-Frank James Jr.

Chapter 5

The Follow Up

One of the questions that I get asked often is "where do leaders make the most mistakes or the most severe mistakes?" My answer over the last several years has held true. Leaders fail at the follow up. Oftentimes leaders become extremely busy and involved, to the point they miss critical areas of checking in and following up. I believe that one of the main reason's leaders fail in this area, is due to their desire to not appear as a micro manager. As an astute learner, I am always looking for ways to improve both myself and ultimately those around me. There are several benefits associated with a simple follow up, but we are going to focus on establishing goals and parameters around the intended end result.

When assigning a project, a clear and concise timeline should be established with a level of flexibility embedded within it. The timeline for when the check in occurs will change according to the completion expectation of the project or assignment, however, the principles remain the same. The first check-in should occur within the first two days. The second at the midway point, and the final check-in, about a week before the project's projected deadline. Let's explore these critical check points and talk about how a gifted leader should navigate the follow up.

It has been my experience that during a project, team members and leaders are the most anxious at the beginning and when approaching the end of a project. It is important to remember that anxiety is a down payment on something negative that has not happened yet. It's like working for a paycheck that you have the right to receive, but yet you believe that if you cash it, it is going to bounce. Divorce that mentality and understand that you get out what you put in. While engaging with your team, it is important to establish a safe and healthy environment which evokes fluid and creative thoughts and ideas. One of the most dynamic things that a leader can do is to encourage ideas from his team members. I have found that individuals work best when their ideas are encouraged and respected, even if they are not implemented. Early check-ins and subsequent follow ups can greatly diminish the anxiety one often encounters at the onset of a new project.

My creativity and innovative thinking often cause others to seek my assistance to launch new ideas. Especially those ideas still in their infancy phase. Not long ago, I was approached by another leader to create a platform that would be utilized throughout his organization. While I was excited to be called upon, I was given no direction. I was provided with an idea and a date of completion. I was told that at some point, I would need to gather insight from other departments within the company as to how best execute the platform integration.

I set out on the journey of completing this project and it wasn't until we reached the testing phase, that it became abundantly clear that this platform we were using would not work. When I shared this revelation with my friend, he asked me "with whom did you test this with and run this by?" I explained that prior to the testing phase; I was in the designing phase and therefore had not checked with anyone.

When you are a leader and tasked with creating something, the check-in and follow up has to occur between both parties. Your time is valuable and completing unapproved tasks can negatively impact the project completion time and stifle your creative ideas. I began to ponder why I had never reached out nor collaborated with other departments. I concluded that it was the "leader credit" that deterred me from checking in with anyone. One thing my mentor taught me was a gifted leader MUST be able to divorce the credit to get to the best result. Initially when he said it, I thought, divorcing the credit was a way for others to "steal my thunder". In actuality, he was really telling me that it's imperative to not be married to an idea so much that you are unwilling to accept correction, enhancements and change. When you are emotionally connected to anything, it's incredibly difficult to step outside of what you are doing to truly get the best end result. Due to the severely rocky start, I needed to activate AR^2 to complete the task. As a gifted leader, it is crucial for you to facilitate meaningful follow up.

As you can probably predict, day one was a bit challenging strictly on the basis of it being a new process. Launch week was very overwhelming, making it impossible to conduct normal follow up. It is important to understand that things can go wrong, even after you have completed all of your checks and balances. It is how you respond to the situation that will determine if you are operating in your gift. Recognizing the importance of efficient and effective follow up, I created an open document. This allowed the team to ask questions as well as view the questions of other team members and my responses. Having this open document also enabled me to anticipate potential future issues and implement a plan of action, which is another example of foresight. Follow up, as you can see, can take on many forms. Keeping in mind that the goal of reciprocal communication must be achieved.

You do not have to be the smartest person in the room to be the leader. Just be the one with the most influence.

NOW GO AND BE GIFTED!

-Frank James Jr.

Chapter 6

Influence

I always find it fascinating that when I observe people watching a roller coaster move along the track that they are shocked that the metal sways a bit. Now logically, that presents a level of uneasiness to people who see this, but I view it a bit differently. While for safety reasons we want and need the metal to be strong, firm and unwavering; it is important to know that if there was no movement of the structure, it would be brittle and could snap and break. When you look at things from a different perspective, it affords you the opportunity to fill in gaps that you may not have known or thought about. This is how a gifted leader must function. Understand that you may not be the expert in the room but surely there is room for you and your gift to flourish. Always remember that when you operate in your gift, you don't have to sit at the head of the table. Wherever you sit, the table will shift.

I have had the esteemed pleasure to sit under a few dynamic Pastors in my life and there is one characteristic that all of them share: influence. Influence refers to the ability to change perspectives in an enforced manner. It is also the ability to be memorable wherever you go. The way you move, the passion behind what you say and the humble authority that you possess shapes not only your influence, but how it is perceived by others. My current Pastor, Apostle Rodney L. Savage Sr., shared this with our leadership team: "one of the major things that set you all apart from others is your level of influence". Initially my response to his statement was confusion. I had witnessed the power of his influence in the past and felt that this characteristic was not within me. He went on to describe attributes of leaders as well as speak to each leadership member. He identified what attributes they brought to the table. When he spoke about me, I remember him saying "Frank, man, people in all states are asking about you. They want to know where you are, what you're doing and when you are coming. They love you; they love being around you and they love receiving from your gift!" Now as you can imagine, I was completely surprised by hearing this because I had never considered being thought of or spoken about in this manner. It is important to note that when you are a leader, most of your everyday interactions consist of directing, giving information and getting results. In considering this, their depiction of me was a surprise. Then I realized they were not only speaking about me as a person, but they were speaking about how I used my gift to navigate the world.

This takes me back to the story from earlier as the GM. I was 26 years old and was afforded the opportunity to take on this large responsibility. When I first started at this park, things were rough. There were so many things that needed to be corrected and changed that I immediately felt overwhelmed. I remember asking the owners in my interview, "Since this is a family-owned business, what is the level of influence that I will have on decision making at the park?" I remember them looking at me with a face that was seemingly perplexed. They asked, "What do you mean?" I informed them of my access requirement needs, which were imperative for the successful achievement of expectations identified within this position. I requested involvement in all major park meetings with a weighted vote and the autonomy to make decisions. I could tell that in that moment, they didn't really know what they had signed up for when hiring me. They merely responded with "let us know what you need and we will see". After internally dissecting their response, I realized it would require a lot of maneuvering to accomplish the desired tasks. So, I set off on a mission to increase my level of influence with the owners. Influence is not really something that you can commission to change, you merely have to show and prove it.

When we think about how we "grade" our country's President, there is something called The First 100 days. Usually within these days, we consider all of the things that have or have not been accomplished as well as the policies that are presented and we make an inference based off of those results. I used a similar approach. My first mission was to tackle the items that the owners identified as extremely important. Naturally, this was to ensure the owners that I clearly understood their concerns and made them a priority. Navigating influence requires a level of submission and authority. Their major concerns were the cost control of the food and the overall cleanliness and condition of the facility. Over the next several weeks, I enlisted 4 different vendors to provide me with new products and pricing.

Tapping into my culinary background, I was able to speak directly to cost control and product flavor with the vendors without the owner's assistance. Once the vendors and I negotiated a reasonable product cost agreement, I invited the owners to indulge in the new products. Their initial thoughts when viewing the products was, "wow, this is a lot of cooked and wasted food and it looks a bit different". After I explained the spread in detail, they began to taste the food and make suggestions. To say they were blown away was quite an understatement. I remember being told, "There is no way that you are getting this food for these prices, are you friends with the vendor?" I laughed and explained to them, when you are knowledgeable in a particular area, you can speak directly to it! This is influence, in its purest form.

At the time I hadn't realized that my gift in leadership was working twofold: with both the owners as well as the food purveyor. My ability to demonstrate effective business sense and a level of authority translated to influence among the owners. The new responses to my recommendations were now, "you tell us what you need Frank, and we will make it happen." It is a leader's dream to be trusted to that magnitude where you can actually exercise and function in your gift. There was a plethora of things that I was able to change strictly based on the fact that my level of influence had risen.

There are certain attributes of a gifted leader that facilitates influence. One attribute that I believe some leaders misunderstand is the idea that leaders are always in control of people. A gifted leader does not control people; they lead environments through vulnerability, transparency, and intentionality, thus gaining great influence. In leadership you must create a safe space where individuals are comfortable openly expressing themselves, failing without judgment and growing without limits! It is that idea of caring from which influence stems. As a gifted leader, your level of influence will cause people to engage no matter where you are or what you do. One of the most valuable things that people possess is their time and it's critical that you never take that for granted. When you have this type of influence, people feel like they are always receiving from your gift. Showing up becomes a byproduct of you simply being yourself.

You cannot call yourself a leader if the machine falls apart in your absence. A gifted leader cultivates the team machine properly and trust their own training. If the team cannot handle it alone, check the leader!

NOW GO AND BE GIFTED!

-Frank James Jr.

Chapter 7

Cultivating Gifts

A truly gifted leader will possess the attitude of leadership; demonstrate vulnerability and transparency amongst their peers, while being intentional with both words and deeds. This leader will understand the necessity to use both empathy and wisdom when making tough choices or having those hard conversations. Gifted Leaders weave regular checkups and follow up into their regular routine, to ensure that both the goals are being met and the staff is heard and respected. Above all else, a truly gifted leader uses their gift to cultivate the gifts of others. As I have told you before, leadership is not only an occupation, but also a gift. Truly gifted leaders walking in their calling are mindful of how they interact with others and they examine both their intent as well as their actions. It is this examination that shapes your character which in turns grants you influence among others. Cultivating the gifts of others will never take place if you do not have their respect. Cultivation does not have to be an elaborate lesson, task, or project. Small, incremental gestures are often the starting points to unlocking and cultivating greater gifts within others. Whenever I send out an email, I include this simple quote: "Make an impact, everyday!" This quote can serve as a window of opportunity for discussions, reflections, or personal confirmations.

In my consideration of a different career path, I contacted a consultant to gain insight on her career process. During our meeting, she expressed the amount of impact my signature quote had on her. She went on to say that there are not many people in the world who actually set out to make an impact. The fact that this was my desire, it set me apart from many individuals whom she has encountered. The meeting was life changing but she made one very profound statement, "We need more people in the world who want to not just exist but to make an impact". When she said that to me, I was floored! I had experienced a feeling of joy that I had never experienced before. It validated my quest to make an impact on others by helping them to cultivate their gifts. It is from this conversion that *The Gifted Leader* was born. From that day forward, I have aspired to always do my best to inspire others and help to cultivate their gifts like this person did for me.

For a gifted leader, creating an atmosphere where gifts are cultivated and nourished is natural. There are some individuals you encounter who give off zeal of excellence, which inspires you to obtain a level of influence and passion in a relentless way. You must understand that being gifted does not equate to being the smartest in the room. As a leader, you should always be learning and growing. Leadership should never be a comparison game. You cannot compare your level of leadership to someone else's because we were all created with our own special gifts within the parameters of leadership.

I relocated my entire family of four on the premise of landing my dream job. Shortly thereafter I found out that the job was less than dreamy as it had become temporary. As the leader of my household, I recognized my duty and secured other employment to ensure my family was taken care of. Immediately my new employer began to recognize my gifts and she apologized for initially putting me in a position that did not nurture my gift. This was rectified and I eventually became her assistant. In my time working with her, I had the opportunity to make some game changing moves and ultimately raised the standards for others working within the area. I passionately believe that had she not made it her business to cultivate me and my gift, I would have truly missed key promotions in my life.

Generally speaking, no one enjoys being around the leader that claims to know everything and never considers anyone else's thoughts, opinions, or ideas. Effective leaders emphasize that everyone matters; always remember that! Failure to demonstrate this will transversely neglect their gifts cultivation and adversely affect your own growth. Limiting others also limits yourself in operating within your gifts as well as receiving from the gifts of others. There is so much power in understanding that the more you help cultivate others, the sharper your skill set becomes. As a leader, you must be willing to share your humanistic qualities too. A living, growing, mistake bound person who also desires to learn. Your gift in leadership should always be sharpened but you make that impossible when you use language that suggests you are either the best or the only. I have been around many leaders who are vision casters but require other leaders to help cultivate their vision.

It has always been my mission to get in the room around other leaders. The way they feed off each other is unmatched. I have left rooms where I felt like I was having an experience that I could not describe. A level of emotion that I had never felt before and motivation that could not be contained. I had the opportunity to speak with a group of supervisors during my employment at one of the Amusement Parks. This group of young leaders were struggling with how to get people to listen and respect them in their young age. I remember starting out the meeting by saying "leadership is many things, an age it is not". I started with that because I really wanted to set the tone of the meeting to help them understand that they were important; young, gifted and important! I went on to tell them "leadership is a gift and not an occupation and the sooner you walk into it, the less you will fight for respect and honor". Through conversation with these leaders, I found the piece of the puzzle they were missing. It was the ability to operate in their gift and dismiss the idea of the position. It was the consensus of the room that just because they were supervisors, respect and subordination was a requirement. Through the process of identifying how they saw themselves and identifying how others saw them, we were able to define their leadership gift which changed the entire perspective of the room. When it finally clicked to them that leadership is a gift and supervisor is merely just a title, their experience as a leader was enhanced. I felt incredibly grateful for the opportunity to be impactful in cultivating a young leader's gift.

When you are responsible for other leaders, it will present some challenges along the way. There are a lot of functions in leadership, and it is important to know and understand that a gifted leader must be fluent, flexible and committed to continually growing. Cultivating gifts is one of the most profound things that a gifted leader can do. It is both fulfilling and rewarding. We can no longer look at leadership as just a position, promotion or status. We must identify the gift within us to connect to the gift in others, so that we can create a better brigade of leaders, one gift at a time. Share your gift of leadership with the world and watch how great of an impact that you make daily. Now go and be gifted!

Leaders, the standard should be set by your actions, not words. The best example of how people should conduct themselves should be you. If your team is in disarray check your actions! It starts and ends with you.

NOW GO AND BE GIFTED!

-Frank James Jr.

Acknowledgements

What a ride this has been! I would be completely remiss if I did not thank and name a few people who have made this journey of mine a complete success!

My Love, my heartbeat, my wife Jenifer - Thank you for being an unwavering support during this entire process. Without question, you jumped right in to support, enhance and keep me grounded. I absolutely love doing life with you and I sincerely thank you for just simply being you!

My Village - To my Mom (Diane) I love you! Thank you for your relentless expectation of excellence. Because of that, I now get to enjoy the fruits of being an author. To my Dad (Frank) I am so grateful for health and healing in our relationship. I had always longed for the boy-dad relationship and I am incredibly happy that we have that now. To my sisters (Toilise, Christina, Keisa) You all already know I love you with every fiber of my being. Even though I am the little brother, I will always be the oldest in my eyes. I will protect y'all always. Thank you for the unwavering support! To all my cousins, aunts, uncles, nieces and nephews, I love you guys so much! First author in the family, not a bad gig! I hope you know now that you can do it too!

My In-Laws (Dawn and Frank) - Look how far we have come? I am so happy that God always knows just how to make things work out for his glory. I am grateful for the two of you every day! Love all to life!

Antasia - Your support, critiques and encouragement has been unmatched. Thank you for your immediate vote of yes when I told you I was thinking about writing a book. I'll never forget you saying, "without question you should write a book, so when are you starting?"

Pecola - From day one you have always been down for Team James and know that I love you forever. Your support goes above and beyond anything that I had ever imagined.

Justin - Great friendships do not happen overnight and we have history that no one can erase. Your constant encouragement and check-ins on this process have truly helped keep me on task and accountable!!

Apostle Rod and Prophet Shavaun - Now y'all know I would not have made it to this moment without you handling my spirit with care. You both have spoken into the life of me and my family from the very first day that we met without you even knowing me. I will never ever forget the many prayers, prophecies, talks and just presence that you both carry in my life. I am eternally grateful for a love example like you two.

Confidence is not an enemy to humility! When you are a gifted leader you make things happen. Shift the energy of any room that you walk into without fear of not being humble. You were created for this!

NOW GO AND BE GIFTED!

-Frank James Jr.

References

Merriam-Webster & Inc. (2019). Merriam-Webster's Collegiate Dictionary, 11th Edition, Jacketed Hardcover, Indexed, 2020 Copyright (11th ed.). MERRIAM-WEBSTER INC.

Brown, B. (2018). Dare to Lead: Brave Work. Tough Conversations. Whole Hearts. (First Edition). Random House.

www.ingramcontent.com/pod-product-compliance
Lightning Source LLC
Chambersburg PA
CBHW060142050426
42448CB00010B/2251